METHOD BOOK 2

LET'S PLAY FLUTE!
FOR BEGINNERS OF ALL AGES

by Elisabeth Weinzierl & Edmund Waechter

To access companion recorded accompaniments online, visit:
www.halleonard.com/mylibrary

Enter Code
3930-4848-8835-8384

If you require a physical CD of the online audio that accompanies this book, please contact Hal Leonard Corporation at info@halleonard.com.

Sy. 2826

RICORDI

HAL•LEONARD® CORPORATION
7777 W. BLUEMOUND RD. P.O. BOX 13819 MILWAUKEE, WI 53213

Original publication: *Flöte Spielen Band B*, by Elisabeth Weinzierl and Edmund Waechter (Sy. 2676)
© 2001 by G. Ricordi & Co.
All rights reserved

English translation/adaptation: *Let's Play Flute! Method Book 2*, by Elisabeth Weinzierl and Edmund Waechter
English translation/adaptation by Richard Laughlin and Rachel Kelly, edited by Rachel Kelly
© 2015 by G. Ricordi & Co.
All rights reserved
Exclusively distributed by Hal Leonard MGB, a Hal Leonard Corporation company.

www.halleonard.com

TABLE OF CONTENTS

The twelve notes of the scale can be played in different registers. In order to distinguish between registers, this method book uses the following system:

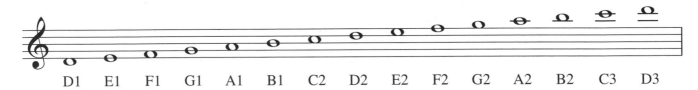

The price of this publication includes access to companion play-along recordings available online, for download or streaming, using the unique code found on the title page. Visit **www.halleonard.com/mylibrary** and enter the access code.

More Fun with Your Flute!

Only a few more new notes to learn and you'll have mastered the entire range from D1–D3, just like those famous French flutists in King Louis XIV's court. You'll soon learn more about one of the court flutists, Jacques Hotteterre "le Romain" and meet more composers and flutists from different eras and countries.

You are already familiar with the lesson structure from Book 1. New notes will be introduced in easy steps with appropriate practice materials. In the songs that follow, you'll have the opportunity to use the notes you just learned. There will be new musical terms introduced, so ask your teacher if you don't understand something or want to know more about it.

Exercise   Exercises present material to help you master various techniques.

Tip   Tips warn about common mistakes, or offer review material from previous lessons.

Activity   Activities indicate exercises that encourage the use of imagination in arranging music, as well as other musical games and ideas.

Most of the songs here are written in two parts so you can play together with your teacher or another student. They'll sound just as good in duet with other instruments, such as violin, oboe, or recorder.

Online Audio

Songs that feature the symbol to the left are recorded and available for download or streaming. To access the companion recordings online, visit: **www.halleonard.com/mylibrary** and enter the code printed on the title page of this book. Here you can listen to each tune as recorded by the authors. If your listening device has a balance switch, you can fade out the top line in the music and play the first flute part alone with the accompaniment.

Before each track begins, there will be some "clicks" to count you in. The little notes under the online audio symbol show you how many such clicks you'll hear.

The first track in the online audio is the tuning note A1 (= 442 hz). Tune up first!

You'll find a number of Christmas and holiday songs at the end of the book, which you can pull out for the appropriate occasion. There's also a fingering chart that displays all the fingerings you've learned. If you've forgotten one or another fingering, you can check the chart for reference.

Chapter 1
New Note: D2

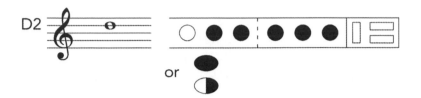

Exercise **Finger Exercises**

Tip Finger connections between D2 and other notes are tricky!

Practice these technical exercises slowly at first and watch your finger movements.

- Lift your right hand little finger from the D♯ key ONLY when playing D2
- Be sure to lift your left hand first finger for D2

Don't forget to focus on producing a good sound despite difficult fingerings!

1. Twinkle, Twinkle, Little Star

French Tune
Arr.: Francois Devienne (1759–1803)

Online
Audio

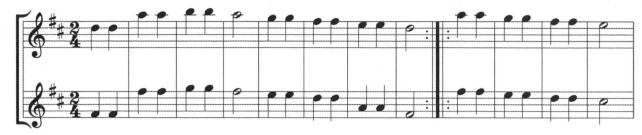

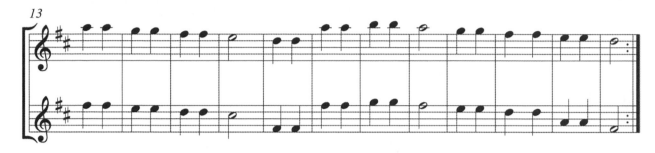

The tune for "Twinkle, Twinkle, Little Star" comes from a French folk song that was popular in the 18th century. Many composers were inspired to arrange the familiar tune. For example, Mozart composed piano variations based on the melody. The same tune is used for "Ba Ba Blacksheep" and "The Alphabet Song."

2. Etude

Giuseppe Gariboldi (1833–1905)

Etudes are pieces that address specific technique problems (such as a difficult fingering). Most etudes are strictly for practice purposes although some are so artistically composed that they become part of the performance repertoire.

Francois Devienne *was a flute professor at the Paris Conservatory when it opened in 1795. The flute methods he composed are still popular today, particularly for their duet material. He composed many other works for flute as well, including concertos, sonatas, duets, and trios.*

The Italian Flutist **Giuseppe Gariboldi** *lived and worked primarily in Paris, where he enjoyed great success with his three operettas and numerous songs. He composed a wealth of etude material covering all levels of difficulty that remain popular today.*

3. Ode to Joy (from Symphony No. 9)

Ludwig van Beethoven (1770–1827)
Arr.: E.W.

Online Audio

Activity You may already be familiar with the tune "Ode to Joy" from the last movement of Beethoven's 9th Symphony. The poem by Friedrich Schiller that Beethoven set to music for this part of the symphony speaks of freedom achieved through brotherly love for all human kind. Let the music inspire you to form a big, luminous sound that fits the idea of the piece.

Exercise   **Finger Exercises**

Tip   **Check:**

- The right hand little finger always presses the D♯ key, except to play D2.
- You must always lift the left hand first finger to open the key for D2.

Activity   If it is the holiday season, you can jump to the Christmas and holiday songs (Nos. 50–55).

4. The Moon Has Risen

Johann Abraham Peter Schulz (1747–1800)

Johann Abraham Peter Schulz *was the orchestra conductor in the royal court of Copenhagen and taught music in Poland and Berlin. His most popular compositions were folk-inspired songs such as the one here, with texts by famous contemporary composers. This and other of his songs remain well known in Germany to this day.*

Tip	**Breath Marks**

Where should you take a breath? Look for appropriate places in the music, mark them with a ❜ and then breathe only in these spots as you play through the piece. It's easy with songs—just sing or recite the lyrics and you'll get a feel for where it's right to take a breath.

5. Come, Follow Me (Canon)

John Hilton (1599–1657)

*The English composer **John Hilton** was the organist for the Church of St. Margaret in Westminister. Like many of his colleagues he wrote canons for entertainment. Back then, it was popular in England to spend one's leisure time singing canons with friends.*

Exercise	**Scale Exercise for Crossing Registers**

Tip	Almost all of the music you'll encounter is built upon scales in different forms or variations. Practicing scales is the foundation of your musical training.

Scale A row of pitches that move step-wise (in seconds) within an octave is a scale. The order of either minor, major, or augmented seconds determines the key. A major scale, for example, consists of five major seconds (**whole steps**) and two minor seconds (**half steps**). The half steps lie between the third and fourth as well as the seventh and eighth scale steps. The C major scale contains no accidentals:

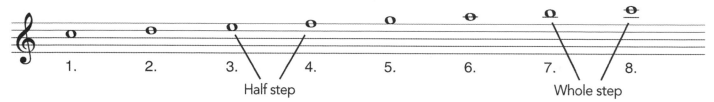

It's easier to view scales on the piano keyboard. The white keys are the tones without accidentals (natural notes). The black keys divide the whole steps into half steps. Notice that E to F (three and four in C Major) is a half step without a black key. B to C (seven and eight in C Major) is also a half step, with no black key in between.

Each natural note can be raised with a sharp (#) or lowered with a flat (♭).

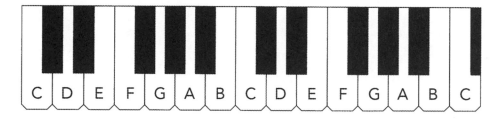

Now use this knowledge to write out some scales yourself. Start with a row of natural tones (try G1 to G2 and F1 to F2) and add accidentals to create half steps between the 3rd and 4th, as well as the 7th and 8th steps. Now you've got the G major scale and the F major scale.

Of course you can also identify those accidentals by ear! Play the G major scale (from G1 to G2) or the F major scale (from F1 to F2). If a note sounds wrong, you just need to raise or lower it. Experiment until your ear recognizes the correct pitches. Which accidentals do we need for G Major? F Major?

Activity ## Ear Training

> Your teacher will play different half and whole step combinations on the flute.
> Can you hear the difference between the two intervals? Sing or play them back.

6. Minuet

Joseph Bodin de Boismortier (1689–1755)

7. Shalom Chaverim (Canon)

Israeli Folk Song

Joseph Bodin de Boismortier *was well known in Paris as a composer of ballet music. He enjoyed his greatest success with his works for flute, as they were easily playable by amateur musicians. He wrote music for one, two, or three flutes, with and without accompaniment, as well as six concertos for five flutes, an uncommon configuration.*

8. Old French Dance

Arr.: E.W.

Online
Audio

| Tip | This dance was notated in an old French tradition using "notes blanches" (white notes), or half notes, which are each one beat. The closing dance in 6/2 time, found in the last two measures of the piece, is to be played faster than the first part of the song: $\frac{4}{2}$ 𝅗𝅥𝅗𝅥 ≙ $\frac{6}{2}$ 𝅗𝅥𝅗𝅥𝅗𝅥 |

| Activity | This dance lends itself to a rhythmic accompaniment on the tambourine. |

9. Melody

Robert Schumann (1810–1856)
Arr.: E.W.

Online
Audio

*As a composer, **Robert Schumann** focused primarily on works for piano and his wife, the virtuoso pianist Clara Wieck Schumann, often performed them. Nevertheless, his symphonies, chamber works, and songs represent some of the most important works of the Romantic era. As was unfortunately the case with many well-known composers of his day, Schumann neglected to write any soloistic flute works.*

10. Allegro

François Devienne (1759–1803)

Staccato, portato, tenuto A dot placed over or under a note means it should be played **staccato,** or detached. Attack the note quickly and clearly with your tongue and immediately interrupt the airstream, making space between neighboring notes. A little burst of air from the lower stomach will give your staccati an elastic, bouncing quality.

If there are no dots or other signs over the notes, you must decide how long the space between the notes should be, taking into consideration the character of the piece.

There is a wide range of possibilities, from the longer notes called **portato** or **tenuto** and notated with a beam or dot and beam, to very short staccati.

11. Pastorale

Bolivian Melody
Arr.: E.W.

Online
Audio

Activity Did you notice that this pastorale (a romanticized image of rural life depicted through music) consists of only five pitches? "**Pentatonic**" is the technical term for such five-note groupings. One can easily write or improvise melodies using only this material. Try extending this melody with an improvised tune of your own, using the five pitches shown below. Bongos or congas would provide a good accompaniment. It will be easier to improvise over a steady 3/4 or 4/4 meter.

In the traditional music of many South American cultures, different types of flutes are used: pan flutes of all sizes, end-blown vertical flutes, recorders, and transverse flutes. It's not uncommon to encounter South American street musicians playing flutes in all corners of the globe.

Photo: A flute player at an Incan Festival of the Sun celebration (Inti Raymi)

(Photo courtesy of Reist Doelf)

Chapter 2
New Note: D♯2/E♭2

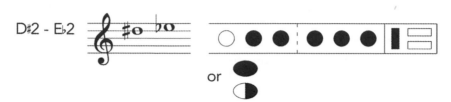

Exercise **Finger Exercises**

12. Air (Song)

Jacques Hotteterre "le Romain" (1673–1763)

Online Audio

Activity Now that you've learned to play E♭2, you can play the next Christmas song, "God Rest Ye Merry, Gentlemen" (No. 53).

Jacques Hotteterre "le Romain" *was the most significant member in a family of woodwind players employed by the French royal court. He was among the first generation of flutists who founded the tradition of the French flute school. A prolific composer, Hotteterre wrote many works for flute, including the first published flute method. Titled* Principes de la Flûte, *it was published in 1707.*

In this painting by André Bouys (1656–1740) we see a group of musicians from the royal court of King Louis XIV (the Sun King). The flutist depicted standing and pointing at the music on the table is most likely Michel de La Barre, seen here to be showing off his latest work *Sonates en trio pour la flûte traversière* (1707). La Barre dedicated these sonatas to the nobleman and amateur flutist Monsieur Landais, who may be the man sitting on the right holding a valuable ivory flute. The central figure of the painting could also be Jacques Hotteterre "Le Romain," however, with his brother Jean in the seat at the right.

Exercise ## Finger Exercises

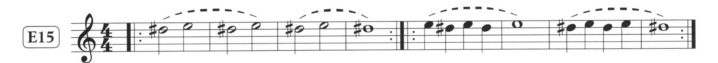

13. Duet

Joseph Bodin de Boismortier (1689–1755)

Tip ### Check!

Make sure your fingering is correct – remember, for D♯2 you should raise the first finger!

14. Go Down, Moses

African American Spiritual
Arr.: E.W.

Exercise   Finger Exercises

Exercise **Scale Exercises**

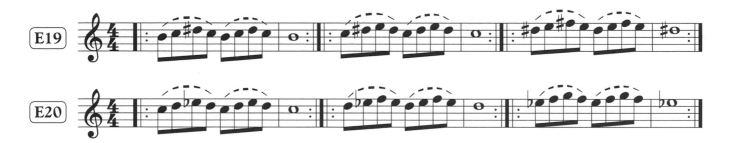

Tip Even when playing a passage with difficult fingering, pay attention to producing a good tone. Use long notes to develop the richness of your tone even further.

15. It's Not the Wind That Rustles

Russian Melody
Arr.: E.W.

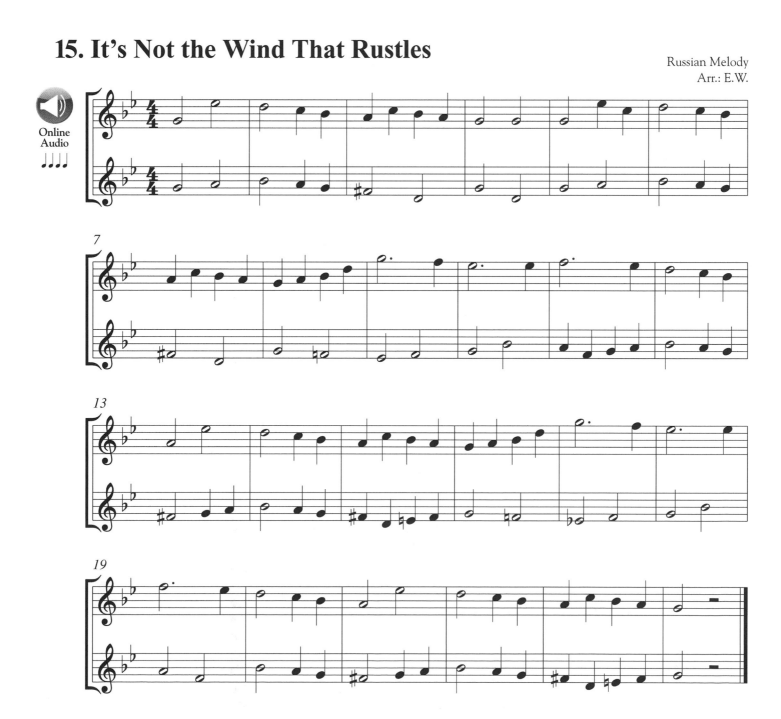

16. All My Thoughts

from the Lochamer Song Book (c1450)

| Tip | Separating measures through the use of bar lines was first introduced about 400 years ago. Before that, rhythmic accents were gleaned from the text and melodic line alone.

17. Andante

Wolfgang Amadeus Mozart (1756–1791)

Andante means "at a walking pace." As opposed to running, we always have at least one foot on the ground when walking. We can translate this musically by using a gentle legato or portato articulation. Even the notes with staccato markings should not be played as short or bouncy as we did in "Allegro" (No. 10).

18. Moderato

Wilhelm Popp (1828–1902)

Online Audio

Dynamics It would be quite boring if we played all music at the same volume all the time! Usually, composers will provide directions for how loud or soft to play in the form of dynamic markings. Dynamic markings are written in Italian, just like the tempo markings we have learned:

f = forte: loud
mf = mezzo forte: medium loud
p = piano: soft
> = accent: emphasize the note

Tip   **piano** – blow less air through a small lip opening while still maintaining a fast airstream.

       forte – use a strong airstream through a larger lip opening (relax lips and loosen jaw)

Different dynamic levels will affect your pitch and sound. A good flutist knows how to compensate for these differences. Listen closely to yourself and correct any fluctuations in your tone or pitch. In Book 1 of *Let's Play Flute!* (pg 8) we learned some techniques while playing on the headjoint alone:

* Extend, contract, or slack the lower lip and lower jaw.
* Rotate the instrument forwards and backwards.
* Raise or lower the head.

Wilhelm Popp, *solo flutist of the Hamburg Philharmonic Orchestra, was an uncommonly diligent composer of music for flute. He turned out over 500 works, including showpieces for virtuosos, tunes for hobby flutists, practice literature, full-scale flute methods, as well as his own arrangements of compositions by other composers.*

Chapter 3
New Note: D1

D1   or

Exercise   **Finger Exercise**

E21

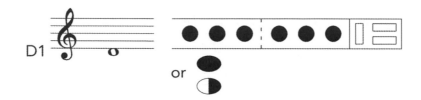

Tip

Watch your right hand little finger as it swings up and down, always moving in the opposite direction of the other fingers.

Exercise   **Octave Exercise**

E22

19. By the Light of the Moon (Au clair de la lune)

French Folk Song

9

20. Oh, How Quiet in the Evening (Canon)

German Melody

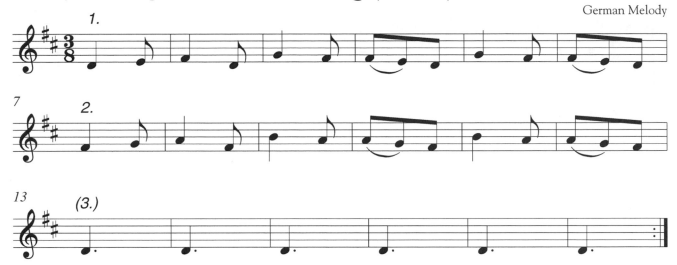

Exercise · Tone Exercise

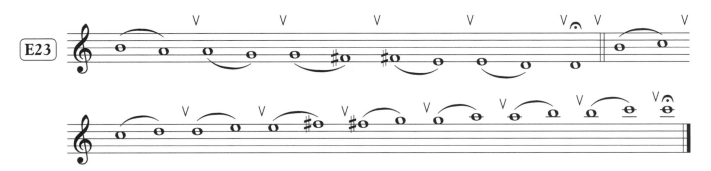

Tip
- Hold the notes out as long as you can while maintaining a good tone.
- Keep your tone consistent throughout the registers!

The flute will tend to sound loud and shrill in the upper register: play softly and gently!

The flute will tend to sound pale and weak in the lower register: play with strength and personality!

21. Michael, Row the Boat Ashore

African American Spiritual

Online Audio ♩♩♩

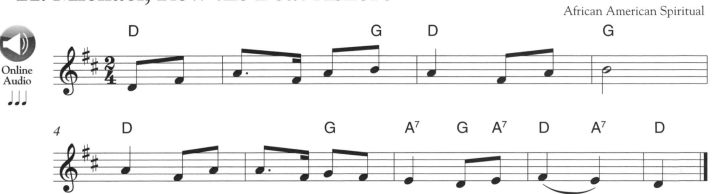

22. Hungarian Folk Song

Arr.: E.W.

Online
Audio

23. Hey, Ho! Nobody Home (Canon)

French Melody

Exercise **Arpeggio Exercises**

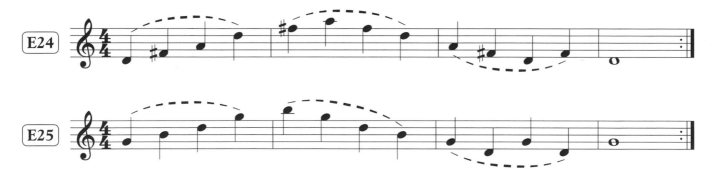

E24

E25

Tip Arpeggios (broken chords) in their various forms provide the essential foundation of a musical composition, along with scales. Make sure your practice routine covers both scale and arpeggio work.

Triads Choose a note out of a scale and skip over its neighbor to the next note. Skip over the note after that to choose a third note. With these three notes you've formed a triad! If you take the 1st, 3rd and 5th steps from the scale, you'll have formed a tonic triad. For example, in C major the tonic triad would be: C, E, and G. Triads are a type of arpeggio.

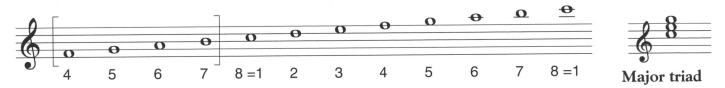

4   5   6   7   8 =1   2   3   4   5   6   7   8 =1   **Major triad**

Activity Build and write out some more triads and arpeggios starting on different steps of the C major scale. The triads commonly found in a musical **cadence** (the last chords of a piece) are the tonic (built from the first scale step), the **subdominant** (built from the fourth step) and the **dominant** (built from the fifth step). Many melodies can be accompanied using just these three chords.

1   2   3   4   5   6   7

In the same manner, you'll construct chords (a triad with all three notes played at the same time) on the G and F Major Scales:

1   2   3   4   5   6   7   1   2   3   4   5   6   7

To hear what you've written down, you'll need a polyphonic instrument such as the piano. Or you could use three flutes. One flute alone cannot play the three tones of the chord simultaneously. Instead, a flutist must arpeggiate the chord by playing the notes separately.

The sound of a chord or triad is determined by the different combinations of minor thirds (an interval of one and a half steps) and major thirds (an interval of two whole steps) it contains.

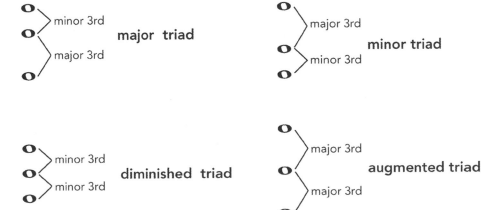

minor 3rd
major triad
major 3rd

major 3rd
minor triad
minor 3rd

minor 3rd
diminished triad
minor 3rd

major 3rd
augmented triad
major 3rd

Activity Ear Training Games

- Your teacher will play a mix of minor and major thirds on the flute (both from top to bottom and bottom to top). Can you hear (without peeking!) the difference in the two intervals? Sing or play them back!
- When you've perfected that, do the same using the three-note arpeggiated triads.
- It's usually more difficult to hear the intervals when the notes are played simultaneously. Try this using a piano or other polyphonic instrument.

24. Yes, I'd Like a Little Violin

August Heinrich Hoffmann von Fallersleben (1798–1874)

25. Oh, Susanna

Stephen Foster (1826–1864)

Online
Audio

26. Gavotte

Nicholas Chédeville (1705–1782)

Nicholas Chédeville *was born into a well-known French musical family who were also related to the Hotteterre family (see page 15). Both Nicholas and his older brother Esprit-Philippe (1696–1762) were members of the Paris Opera Orchestra and wrote a number of compositions for flute.*

Chapter 4
New Note: D#1/E♭1

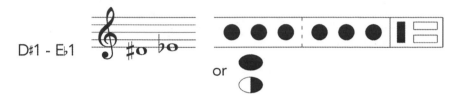

D#1 - E♭1

Exercise **Finger Exercise**

E26

Octave Exercise

E27

Arpeggio Exercise

E28

Tone Exercise

E29

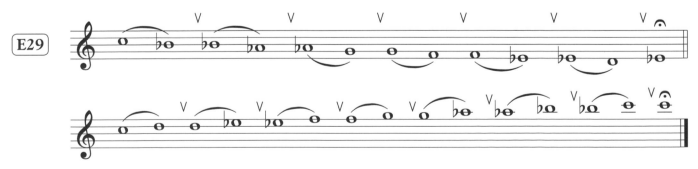

Activity Now you know all the notes you need to play the Christmas song "Still, Still, Still" (No. 54) as well as "Auld Lang Syne" (No. 55) for the New Year.

27. The Little Humpbacked Man

German Melody from Holstein

28. The Rakes of Mallow

Irish Song

In Ireland, the flute is a beloved folk instrument in several different forms, from the tin whistle to the Boehm flute. Flute bands in Ireland are as prevalent as wind bands in other cultures. The world-renowned Northern Irish flutist James Galway spent his youth playing in a flute band.

29. Brahms' Lullaby

Johannes Brahms (1833–1897)

Johannes Brahms *was one of the Romantic era's greatest composers. He wrote four symphonies, violin and piano concertos,* Ein deutsches Requiem (A German Requiem), *chamber music, solo piano pieces, and* Lieder *(art songs). His orchestral works feature beautiful solo passages for flute, but unfortunately he didn't write works specifically for the flute as a solo instrument.*

Chapter 5
New Note: D3

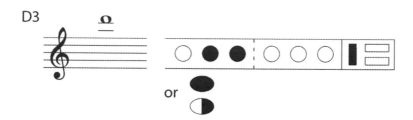

Exercise **Finger Exercise**

Octave Exercise

Scale Exercise in Triplets

Triplet A triplet consists of three tones grouped together whose length corresponds to that of two duple notes:

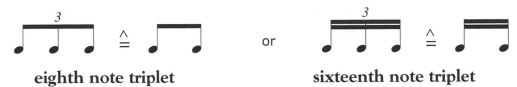

eighth note triplet   or   **sixteenth note triplet**

Activity   • Always practice new rhythms by clapping, singing, or speaking.

Look - at - the   new - note   look - at - the   song

• Tap your foot on each beat!
• Make up your own words to other rhythms that use triplets!

30. Hava nagila

Jewish Folk Song
Arr.: E.W.

Online
Audio

31. Adagio

Jean-Baptiste Loeillet de Gant (1688–c1720)

Online
Audio

Adagio slow

*Three members of the **Loeillet** family from Gent (a city in contemporary Belgium) all worked contemporaneously as flutists and oboists, and as composers of chamber music for woodwinds. Jean-Baptiste (1680–1730) lived in London. His brother Jacques (1685–1746) was a musician in the royal courts of Munich and Versailles. Their cousin Jean-Baptiste (nicknamed "de Gant") lived in Holland and France.*

32. Etude

Ernesto Köhler (1849–1907)

Moderato

 **Tip**   ## Checklist for tricky fingerings:

- Practice slowly and concentrate! Increase tempo gradually.
- Work in small segments!
- **D2**: raise your left hand first finger!
- **E2** (and all notes other than **D2**): your right hand little finger presses the D♯ key.
- Make up your own exercises to help master tricky passages!

33. Old Man Quinn

Irish Tune

Ernesto Koehler *was born in Modena, Italy, where his father was a flutist in the ducal court. In his youth, Ernesto was already well known throughout Europe as a flute virtuoso. He was the solo flutist in an orchestra in Vienna and later in St. Petersburg. Of his over one hundred compositions, his romantic etudes, played by many students learning the flute, are the best known.*

34. Fifty Dollars (from the *Peasant Cantata*)

Johann Sebastian Bach (1685–1750)
Arr.: E.W.

Online
Audio

35. La Jesusita

Mexican Melody
Arr.: E.W.

Online
Audio

D.S. al ⊕ - ⊕   D.S. = Dal segno (from the sign). After reaching the end of a piece, jump back to this sign 𝄋 and continue on to the coda sign ⊕, finally jumping to the second coda sign ⊕ to complete the piece.

36. It Sounds So Splendid (from *The Magic Flute*)

Wolfgang Amadeus Mozart (1756–1791)
Arr.: Johann Baptist Wendt (1745–1801)

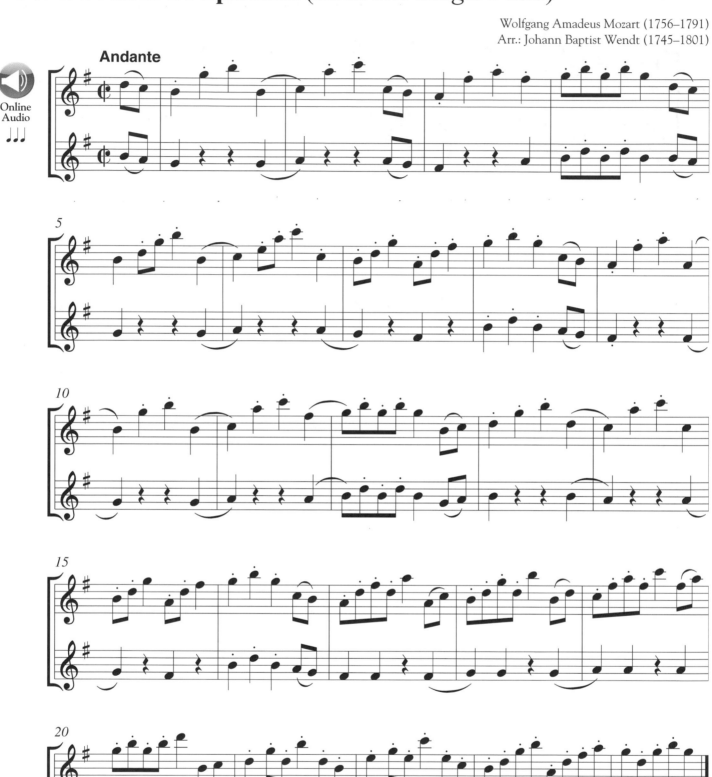

| Tip | Combining a short tongue attack with pulses of air from the lower stomach will enable you to mimic the sound of the glockenspiel (for which this melody was originally written). You can practice this using a "diaphragm staccato" system where each tone is produced only through air impulses (without tonguing!). Work toward developing a clear and consistent attack on each note. |

Chapter 6
New Notes: C♯2/D♭2 and C♯3/D♭3

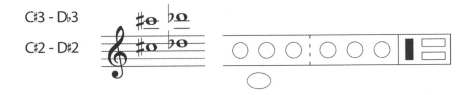

Exercise | **Finger Exercise**

Tip | The notes C♯/D♭ have the same fingering in both octaves (like the notes we learned in *Let's Play Flute!* Method Book 1). However, this fingering presents some difficulties:

- You can't stabilize the flute as before with the fingers of the left hand. If your instrument wobbles or you experience too much pressure on your lips, it's time to check your playing posture and the position of the head joint to re-establish proper balance.

- C♯2/D♭2 (not C♯3/D♭3) can often sound thin and sharp. We can improve the tone by employing a faster air stream that is directed slightly downwards. Try to adjust the sound as if you were singing it through your nose.

37. Minuet

Michel Blavet (1700–1768)

Online Audio

Michel Blavet *was the principal flutist in the Paris Opera Orchestra, and according to many sources he was the premier flutist of his time. As one story goes, Blavet taught a royal prince whose dog would bark and whimper when the prince played the flute. When Blavet played, however, the dog was silent! The prince's playing must not have been to his dog's liking. Today, Blavet's sonatas, duets and concertos for flute are mainstays of the flute repertoire.*

38. Andante

Heinrich Soussmann (1796–1848)

Heinrich Soussmann *was a flutist from Berlin. Following a successful concert tour to St. Petersburg he was hired as principal flutist of the opera orchestra there. Later on, Soussmann became the musical director of the city's Royal Theatre. His melodic etudes for flute remain popular to this day.*

39. Adagio

Johann Joachim Quantz (1697–1773)

Johann Joachim Quantz began his career as oboist in the royal court of August II the Strong in Dresden. He became increasingly enthralled with the French school of flute, however, and decided to shift his focus there. Quantz studied with Pierre Gabriel Buffardin, a colleague in Dresden and sought inspiration through Blavet's artistic legacy in Paris. The Prussian Crown Prince (later King) Frederick the Great, an excellent flutist in his own right and composer of 120 sonatas and four concertos for flute, chose Quantz as his teacher and hired him as a court musician.

Quantz's method book *On Playing the Flute* was published in 1752. It describes in detail how the music of the day was to be played and is more famous than the over 300 flute concertos and other flute works that Quantz wrote in the late Baroque galant style. In his chapter on Adagio, Quantz states: "In order to master the adagio, one must adopt a calm, almost melancholy state of mind, so that the emotional state of the performer is the same as the composer who wrote it…for that which does not come from the heart does not easily reach the heart."

Adolf von Menzel (1815–1905) conducted intense historical research in order to create an accurate portrayal in the above painting, *The Flute Concerto*. It depicts the Prussian King Frederick the Great performing at his Sanssouci Castle in Potsdam. Johann Joachim Quantz, his teacher and court flutist, is depicted on the right. He was the only audience member allowed to applaud when the King played well! In the painting we can spot more court musicians who composed works for flute, such as Carl Philipp Emmanuel Bach (Johann Sebastian's son) accompanying on the harpsichord. The court's principal violinist Franz Benda stands in front of Quantz, and to the left behind the King you can see his two sisters, Wilhelmine of Bayreuth and Amalia of Prussia, who also composed. Standing behind them is the conductor of the Berlin Court Opera, Carl Heinrich Graun.

Quantz also built flutes and was responsible for many innovations in their construction. At the time, flutes were primarily built out of wood, had four inter-connecting parts, and **D1** was their lowest note. The flutes also had a D♯ key as one of up to four available key mechanisms, an adjustable tuning cork (Quantz's invention), and a set of extending middle joints to accommodate various tuning systems. Unlike previous instruments (remember the pictures of the Praetorious model flutes?) and today's Boehm flutes, these Baroque flutes featured a reversed conical bore whereby the inner diameter decreased from top to bottom like that of a recorder. Today, many artists prefer to perform period music on reproductions of these older models. Maybe you'll have a chance to hear them online, on a recording, or in concert. Do you hear the difference between the Baroque flute and your Boehm flute?

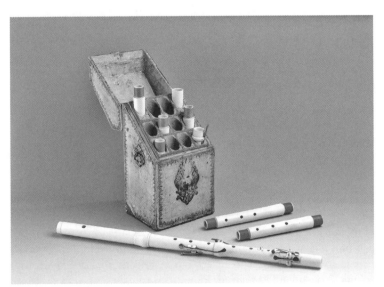

Photo left: This is a rare and valuable example of one of Frederick the Great's flutes, built out of ivory and including a set of exchangeable pipes. It also features one of Quantz's innovations, the foot joint with two separate keys for D♯ and E♭.

40. Andante

Joseph Haydn (1732–1809)

Online
Audio

| **Dolce** | sweetly, delicately |

| **Cresc. / crescendo** | increasing in volume, often indicated with this sign: |

| **Dim. / diminuendo** or **Decr. / decrescendo** | decreasing in volume, often indicated with this sign: |

Joseph Haydn *was one in a group of Viennese composers from the Classical era who made a distinct impression on the music of their time. He was a friend and advisor of Mozart's and gave Beethoven composition lessons. His symphonies, piano sonatas, and chamber works are played regularly on classical radio stations, featured on many recordings, and often included on concert programs. Some of his trios and quartets feature the flute. Many of his works were arranged for the flute during Haydn's lifetime. The Andante above is one example, which is a movement from one of his string quartets. One work often attributed to Haydn, the Concerto in D Major for Flute, was actually penned by his lesser-known colleague Leopold Hoffmann.*

41. **Andante grazioso** (from Sonata KV 331)

Wolfgang Amadeus Mozart (1756–1791)

Arr.: E.W.

Online Audio

Grazioso gracefully, charmingly

sf or **sfz** **sforzato**: strongly accented

A wedge or line placed vertically over a note often means staccato, just like the dot symbol we learned about in Method Book 1. In some cases, wedges and lines indicate a more distinct separation (staccatissimo) with accent.

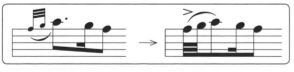 The smaller notes in bar 10 are known as grace notes, which are usually played on the beat. Grace notes have no metered value of their own. Their value is deducted from a neighboring (usually the following) note, as demonstrated in the example at left.

Exercise **Finger Exercise**

E34

42. Rigaudon

Joseph Bodin de Boismortier (1689–1755)

Online
Audio

Tip   Phrasing

Don't forget to add breath marks to each piece you practice! This will help you to coordinate your breath to the musical phrase, just like in everyday speech. In the song above, you'll surely find the appropriate places to breathe. Watch out: pick up notes are always part of the following phrase!

43. Bosom of Abraham (Canon)

Gospel Song

Finger Exercises

Exercise

44. Andante

August Eberhard Mueller (1767–1817)

August Eberhard Mueller *was born in Hannover and served as cantor of the Thomaskirche (St. Thomas Church) in Leipzig, where Johann Sebastian Bach spent the majority of his career. He was also an accomplished flutist who published two methods for flute as well as many compositions and arrangements for the instrument, including twenty-three duets.*

45. Moderato

Kaspar Kummer (1795–1870)

46. Andantino

Armand Vanderhagen (1753–1822)

Armand Vanderhagen *was born in Antwerp. He later worked in Paris as a clarinetist and composer. He mostly wrote music for clarinet, but he also composed for flute and oboe. His works were mainly aimed at students and amateur players.*

Exercise   ## Scale Exercise in Triplets

Tip   This exercise is written in the key of D major (with F♯ and C♯). Transpose it to other keys such as C major (no accidentals), A major (with F♯,C♯,G♯) or E♭ major (with B♭,E♭,A♭). Begin each transposition on the tonic note (for example, C2 for C major in bar 4) and play the exercise from there. When you've reached the last bar, jump to the beginning and play through to where you started.

47. Minuet

George Frideric Handel (1685–1759)

George Frideric Handel *was one of the most important composers in the Baroque era. He began his career as an organist in Halle, his hometown in Germany. He enjoyed later success in Hamburg with his operas before relocating to Italy for further study of Italian music. Handel finally moved to London, where he spent the majority of his career and composed his most famous works (Water Music, Music for the Royal Fireworks, Messiah). Handel also wrote several sonatas that became standard repertoire for flutists. This minuet is from the Sonata in G Major.*

48. Dear Old Stockholm

Swedish Folk Song
Arr.: E.W.

Online
Audio

49. In Bahia

Brazilian Melody
Arr.: E.W.

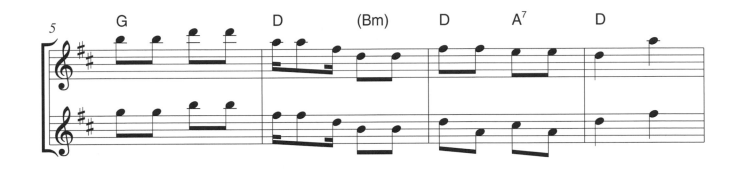

Christmas and Holiday Songs

These songs can be played after finishing Chapter 1

50. While By My Sheep

German Carol
Arr.: E.W.

Online
Audio

51. O Sanctissima

Sicilian Carol
Arr.: E.W.

Online
Audio

This song can be played after finishing Chapter 1

52. Silent Night

German Carol
Arr.: Rachel Kelly

**Online
Audio**

This song can be played after finishing Chapter 2

53. God Rest Ye Merry, Gentlemen

English Carol
Arr.: Rachel Kelly

This song can be played after finishing Chapter 4

54. Still, Still, Still

Austrian Carol

Online
Audio
♩♩

This song can be played after finishing Chapter 4

55. Auld Lang Syne

Scottish Folk Melody
Arr.: Rachel Kelly

Online
Audio
♩♩♩

Fingering Chart

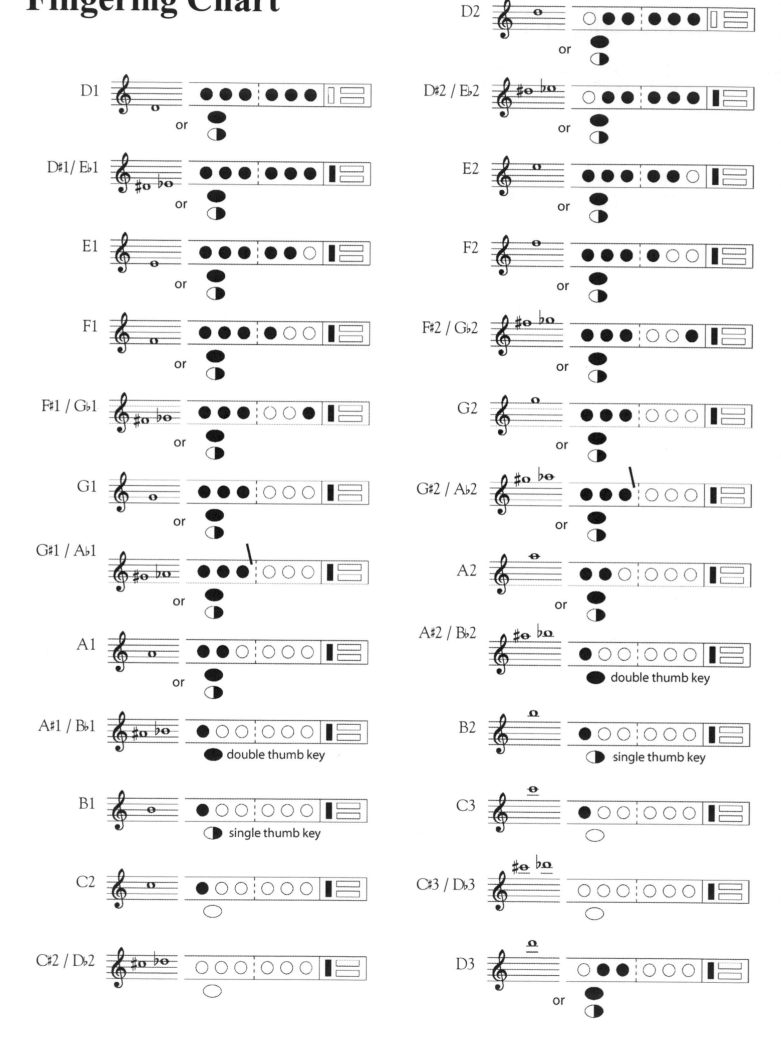

Alphabetical Song Index

Index of Musical Concepts and Terms

On the recording

Musicians on the Recordings:

Elisabeth Weinzierl   (Flute, Harpsichord)

Edmund Waechter   (Flute)

Felix Gargerle   (Violin)

Christiane Arnold   (Viola)

Udo Hendrichs   (Cello)

Eva Schieferstein   (Piano)

Ladia Base   (Piano)

Paul Tietze   (Electric Bass)

Werner Schmitt   (Drums, Percussion)

Farao Studio, Munich
Sound Engineer: Robert F. Schneider

Musicians on Songs 52, 53, and 55:

Emily M. Koi   (Flute)

Andrea Pelloquin   (Flute)

Tanner-Monagle, Inc., Milwaukee
Sound Engineer: Eric Probst

What's next?

Now that you've finished the book, go back and review your favorite tunes. You'll find that you can play many of them better than before. Chances are, you'll fly through some of the pieces that were difficult at the outset. This should show you how quickly you've advanced on the flute. Congratulations!

Using the notes you've learned, try playing all the melodies you know by ear. Choose a different starting note for each run-through and use the appropriate register.

We wish you continued fun and success with your flute!

Flutists Elisabeth Weinzierl and Edmund Wächter both reside in Munich, Germany and are well known for their many concerts and workshops throughout Europe and the USA, as well as for their recordings for radio and on CD. Their pedagogic work as flute teachers has led many students to become professional musicians and music teachers. Elisabeth is a professor of flute and flute methodology at the University of Music and Performing Arts in Munich (Hochschule für Musik und Theater München), and Edmund teaches flute and flute methodology at the Ludwig Maximilian University of Munich (Ludwig-Maximilians-Universität).